W9-AFT-282

cloverleaf books™

My Healthy Habits

Keep Calm!

My Stress-Busting Tips

Gina Bellisario

illustrated by Renée Kurilla

M MILLBROOK PRESS · MINNEAPOLIS

For my big brother, Steven —G.B.

For my incredibly supportive
parents who, like Anna's, know just
how to keep me calm in moments of
worry —R.K.

Millbrook Press
A division of Lerner Publishing Group, Inc.
241 First Avenue North
Minneapolis, MN 55401 U.S.A.

Website address: www.lernerbooks.com

Main body text set in Slappy Inline 18/28.
Typeface provided by T26.

Library of Congress Cataloging-in-Publication Data

Bellisario, Gina.
    Keep calm! : my stress-busting tips / by Gina Bellisario ;
illustrated by Renée Kurilla.
        pages   cm. — (Cloverleaf books™ — My healthy habits)
    Includes index.
    ISBN 978-1-4677-1354-2 (lib. bdg. : alk. paper)
    ISBN 978-1-4677-2533-0 (eBook)
    1. Stress management—Juvenile literature. 2. Stress
management for children—Juvenile literature. 3. Anxiety—
Juvenile literature. I. Kurilla, Renée, illustrator. II. Title.
RA785.B45 2014
155.9'042—dc23   2013018077

Manufactured in the United States of America
1 – BP – 12/31/13

TABLE OF CONTENTS

Chapter One

Too Many Worries

My name's Anna. I'm the goalie for my soccer team. Today's game day! First, I have to finish my math homework. And my spelling homework. They're both due tomorrow.

Uh-oh. What if I'm not done in time?

Math + Spelling + Soccer = **STRESS.**

Mom says **stress** is something we feel. She says it comes from being **worried**.

My family members have different worries. But we all feel stress.

Everyone has worries. Take time to figure out yours. That's the first step to dealing with stress.

Mom worries about keeping my little sister, Aimee, safe. Dad worries about being late for work.

Having **a lot to do** makes me worry.

Mom says my schedule is busy.
On Mondays, I play soccer.
On Wednesdays, I take piano
lessons.

But I also have homework and chores.

Stress adds up!

Every activity comes with responsibilities. Try not to sign up for too many activities at a time. Fewer responsibilities equal fewer worries.

Chapter Two

Time Out for Bad Stress

Dad says some worrying is okay. It gives us good stress. Good stress is helpful.

Worrying about a test makes us study.

We try our best. Then the stress goes away.

Good-bye, stress!

Dad says if we keep worrying, good stress can **turn bad**.

Bad stress harms our body.
Our head and stomach hurt.

We feel tired.

Stress can even make us forgetful.

Is my spelling test tomorrow?

When we worry, our bodies make a special chemical. The chemical is called adrenaline. It boosts our energy. But too much adrenaline wears us down. It stops our bodies from relaxing.

Bad stress puts me in a bad mood.

Last week, I worried about finishing my book report. Aimee wanted to play. But I yelled, "Leave me alone!"

I was really sorry. I gave my bad stress a time-out.

Being worried can change our mood. It can make us mad, scared, or shy. We also do things we don't usually do. We bite our nails. We cry about going to school. Taking time for fun helps us feel happy again.

Chapter Three

Game Time!

Phew. My homework is **D-O-N-E**. Game time!

Playing soccer helps my stress go away. So does reading or watching my favorite TV shows. Hanging out with friends does too!

Want to beat stress? Exercise. Eat fruits, vegetables, and other healthy foods. Do something nice for someone. You can also try positive talk. Instead of saying "I can't," say "I can." Cheer yourself on— and cheer up!

Mom says keeping our worries inside makes stress grow. Talking about our worries is healthier.

My family and I have dinner talk. We share how our day went. When someone has a problem, we solve it together.

Dinner talk ends with a hug. Then dessert!

Some families have busy schedules. They can't always eat dinner together. If your family's schedule is busy, plan a different time to talk. How about at breakfast or before bed? After you talk, share a hug too.

Do you worry about getting into trouble? Fitting in? Trying something new? These worries add up to stress.

Talk about your worries. Make time for fun. Shrink your stress—and stay healthy!

Take a Belly Breath

Do you belly breathe? To belly breathe means to breathe deeply. When we take a deep breath, our bodies make endorphins. Endorphins are chemicals that help us feel good. They also calm us down if we are worried. That way, we are ready to solve a problem. Want to relax? Try breathing out your stress with a belly breath.
Here's how:

1) Pretend that a balloon is inside your belly. Put your hands on your belly where the balloon would be.

2) Close your mouth. Through your nose, breathe in and blow up the balloon. In your head, slowly count 1, 2, 3 as you breathe. Feel your belly push out and become round.

3) Using your mouth, let out the air from the balloon. Slowly count 1, 2, 3, 4, 5 inside your head as you blow out. Try to let out the air little by little, not all at once. Feel your belly become flat.

4) Fill and empty your balloon three more times. Breathe in, and count to three. Breathe out, and count to five. By taking belly breaths, you're filling your body with feel-good endorphins. Doesn't that feel great?

Belly-breathing tip: Want to be a belly-breathing expert? Practice breathing out slowly. Take in a belly breath. Then hold a pinwheel in front of your mouth. Count to five while slowly blowing out. Try to keep the pinwheel spinning until you finish counting. If you don't have a pinwheel, use a light object such as a cotton ball or a feather. Place the object on a table. Blow at the object, and try to keep it moving for five seconds.

GLOSSARY

adrenaline: a chemical that our body makes to boost energy

endorphins: chemicals our body makes that help us feel good

exercise: an activity that a person or an animal does to stay healthy

goalie: a player who protects his or her team's goal

mood: how a person is feeling, such as sad, happy, or angry

positive: cheerful

responsibilities: tasks or chores that a person is expected to do

schedule: a plan of things to do

stress: a feeling of worry or pressure

BOOKS

Denshire, Jayne. *Rest and Sleep.* Mankato, MN: Smart Apple Media, 2011.
Learn how resting your body can help make stress go away.

Pett, Mark, and Gary Rubinstein. *The Girl Who Never Made Mistakes.* Naperville, IL: Sourcebooks Jabberwocky, 2011.
Read about Beatrice Bottomwell, a girl who worries about being perfect. Find out how making a mistake helps her feel better.

Salzmann, Mary Elizabeth. *Taking Time to Relax.* Edina, MN: Sandcastle, 2004.
Photos in this book show many ways to relax. See kids playing games, reading stories, and more.

WEBSITES

BAM! Body and Mind
http://www.bam.gov/index.html
Do you feel stress? Take the stress-o-meter quiz from the Centers for Disease Control and Prevention, and find out!

KidsHealth
http://kidshealth.org/kid/
Visit this website to learn what causes stress, and get tips on how to worry less.

Sesame Street
http://www.sesamestreet.org/playlists#media/playlist_372
Sing the "Can Do" song with Bob from *Sesame Street*, and shrink your worries by cheering yourself on.

LERNER SOURCE
Expand learning beyond the printed book. Download free, complementary educational resources for this book from our website, www.lernerresource.com.